HULK VS. THOR
BANNER OF WAR

HULK VS. THOR

BANNE

BRUCE BANNER, more convinced than ever of the damage his presence causes those around him, wants nothing more than to fly the Starship Hulk as far away from civilization as possible. But Banner is accused of murdering a bar full of patrons in El Paso, Texas, and the Avengers are determined to bring him to justice.

Meanwhile, **THOR** has been dealing witl one reality-threatening problem afte another, and he is consumed with anger a his father, who he blames for many of those problems. And now even after his fathe died in battle, Thor finds he can't escape him, as Odin's spirit now inhabits Mjolnir

So Thor is eager to find a release for al this pent-up aggression. Thankfully, he is about to...

COLLECTION EDITOR **JENNIFER GRÜNWALD** || ASSISTANT EDITOR **DANIEL KIRCHHOFFER**
ASSISTANT MANAGING EDITOR **MAIA LOY** || ASSOCIATE MANAGER, TALENT RELATIONS **LISA MONTALBANO**
VP PRODUCTION & SPECIAL PROJECTS **JEFF YOUNGQUIST**
BOOK DESIGNER **ANTHONY GAMBINO** || SENIOR DESIGNER **ADAM DEL RE**
SVP PRINT, SALES & MARKETING **DAVID GABRIEL** || EDITOR IN CHIEF **C.B. CEBULSKI**

HULK VS. THOR: BANNER OF WAR. Contains material originally published in magazine form as HULK VS. THOR: BANNER OF WAR ALPHA (2022) #1, THOR (2020) #25-26 and HULK (2021) #7-8. First printing 2022. ISBN 978-1-302-94663-0. Published by MARVEL WORLDWIDE, INC., a subsidiary of MARVEL ENTERTAINMENT, LLC. OFFICE OF PUBLICATION 1290 Avenue of the Americas, New York, NY 10104. **Printed in Canada.** KEVIN FEIGE, Chief Creative Officer; DAN BUCKLEY, President, Marvel Entertainment; DAVID BOGART, Associate Publisher & SVP of Talent Affairs; TOM BREVOORT, VP, Executive Editor; NICK LOWE, Executive Editor, VP o Content, Digital Publishing; DAVID GABRIEL, VP of Print & Digital Publishing; SVEN LARSEN, VP of Licensed Publishing; MARK ANNUNZIATO, VP of Planning & Forecasting; JEF YOUNGQUIST, VP of Production & Special Projects; ALEX MORALES, Director of Publishing Operations; DAN EDINGTON, Director of Editorial Operations; RICKEY PURDIN, Director o Talent Relations; JENNIFER GRÜNWALD, Director of Production & Special Projects; SUSAN CRESPI, Production Manager; STAN LEE, Chairman Emeritus. For information regardin advertising in Marvel Comics or on Marvel.com, please contact Vit DeBellis, Custom Solutions & Integrated Advertising Manager, at vdebellis@marvel.com. For Marvel subscriptio inquiries, please call 888-511-5480. **Manufactured between 8/5/2022 and 9/6/2022 by SOLISCO PRINTERS, SCOTT, QC, CANADA.**

HULK has recently undergone a dramatic transformation. His alter ego, Bruce Banner, has somehow managed to split the Hulk into three distinct parts: The Hulk's body has been turned into a starship. Banner's psyche pilots it from within the Hulk's mind. And the Hulk's psyche fuels the starship with his anger, which Banner harnesses by locking the Hulk in the "Engine Room" and sending escalating levels of opponents for him to fight.

THOR is the king of Asgard, having recently taken over for his father, Odin. He is struggling to balance his role as the All-Father with his role as one of Earth's mightiest heroes on the Avengers.

DONNY CATES WITH
DANIEL WARREN JOHNSON (HULK #8)
WRITERS

MARTIN COCCOLO
ARTIST

MATT WILSON
COLOR ARTIST

VC'S JOE SABINO (ALPHA, THOR #25-26)
& CORY PETIT (HULK #7-8)
LETTERERS

GARY FRANK &
BRAD ANDERSON
COVER ARTISTS

JAY BOWEN
LOGO DESIGNER

KAITLYN LINDTVEDT &
MICHELLE MARCHESE
ASSISTANT EDITORS

WIL MOSS WITH
ALANNA SMITH
EDITORS

HULK CREATED BY
STAN LEE & **JACK KIRBY**

THOR CREATED BY
STAN LEE, **LARRY LIEBER**
& **JACK KIRBY**

HULK VS. THOR: BANNER OF WAR ALPHA

BANNER OF WAR PART ONE

ETINGS. AM THE TCHER.
MY SWORN DUTY...IS TO WITNESS AND CATALOG SUCH... SEISMIC EVENTS THAT WOULD SHAPE AND ALTER THE COURSE OF HISTORY ITSELF.
I AM CALLED UATU.
AND I AM HERE TO BEAR WITNESS TO THE GREATEST BATTLE THAT ANY WORLD HAS EVER KNOWN. A BATTLE BETWEEN TWO LEGENDARY AND UNBREAKABLE FOES...
THE MIGHTY THOR. AND THE INCREDIBLE HULK.
THESE TWO LEVIATHANS HAVE FOUGHT IN THE PAST, THIS IS TRUE...
BUT NOT LIKE THIS.
NO. THIS TIME...RAGE AND THUNDER SHALL COLLIDE IN A WAR SO BRILLIANT AND AWESOME THAT STORIES OF IT WILL BE SUNG FOR UNTOLD MILLENNIA.
MAKE NO MISTAKE-- THIS...
...THIS IS A BATTLE UNLIKE ANY YOU HAVE EVER SEEN.
BUT FIRST...
ALLOW ME TO BRING YOU UP TO SPEED, AS IT WERE...

"AFTER THE WAR OF THE REALMS, ODIN GAVE THE CROWN AND THRONE OF ASGARD TO HIS SON THOR.
"IN HIS BRIEF TIME AS KING, THOR HAS BEEN MET WITH CHALLENGES THAT WOULD HAVE BENT LESSER BEINGS TO THEIR KNEES.
"IN THE BEGINNING... THERE WAS GALACTUS
"AND THEN THERE WERE THE VISIONS. OF THE MAD TITAN...OF THE ENTROPY OF EXISTENCE...
"...AND THEN...THE CRUELEST OF ALL OF THE THUNDER KING'S TRIALS...
"...THE POSSESSION OF MJOLNIR BY THE BILLION RAGING SOULS OF THE MANGOG...
"A BATTLE WON...BUT AT A GREAT PRICE. MJOLNIR SHATTERED.
"AND ODIN...THOR'S FATHER AND THE FORMER RULER OF THE LAND OF ASGARD...
"...LAY DEAD IN THOR'S VERY ARMS.
"BUT...NOT GONE.
"ODIN'S SOUL BECAME TRAPPE IN MJOLNIR ITSELF.
"SPEAKING IN A VOICE THAT ONLY THOR CAN HEAR.

"...AND THE DIRE REVELATIONS THAT LAY WITHIN THE ENTITY THAT CALLED ITSELF THE *BLACK WINTER*...
"IN THE END, THOR DESTROYED GALACTUS IN A GRAND ACT OF DEFIANCE.
"HE ALSO KILLED THE BLACK WINTER. OR... SO HE THOUGHT...
"(THAT FATE IS NOT FOR ME TO SPEAK OF AND IS A TALE FOR ANOTHER TIME...)
"...THE EMERGENCE OF THE GOLDEN SHADOW--OF DONALD BLAKE, DRIVEN MAD AND TRAPPED. NOW CHAINED FOREVER UPON THE ROCK OF ETERNITY...
"AND SO IT WAS...THAT A GRIEVING, VENGEFUL KING WAS TOLD BY HIS RAVENS THAT THE *HULK* HAD BEEN FOUND IN A LAND FAR FROM THOSE THAT HE HAD KNOWN.
"A TIMELY GIFT FOR A GOD IN DESPERATE NEED OF SOMETHING TO HIT.

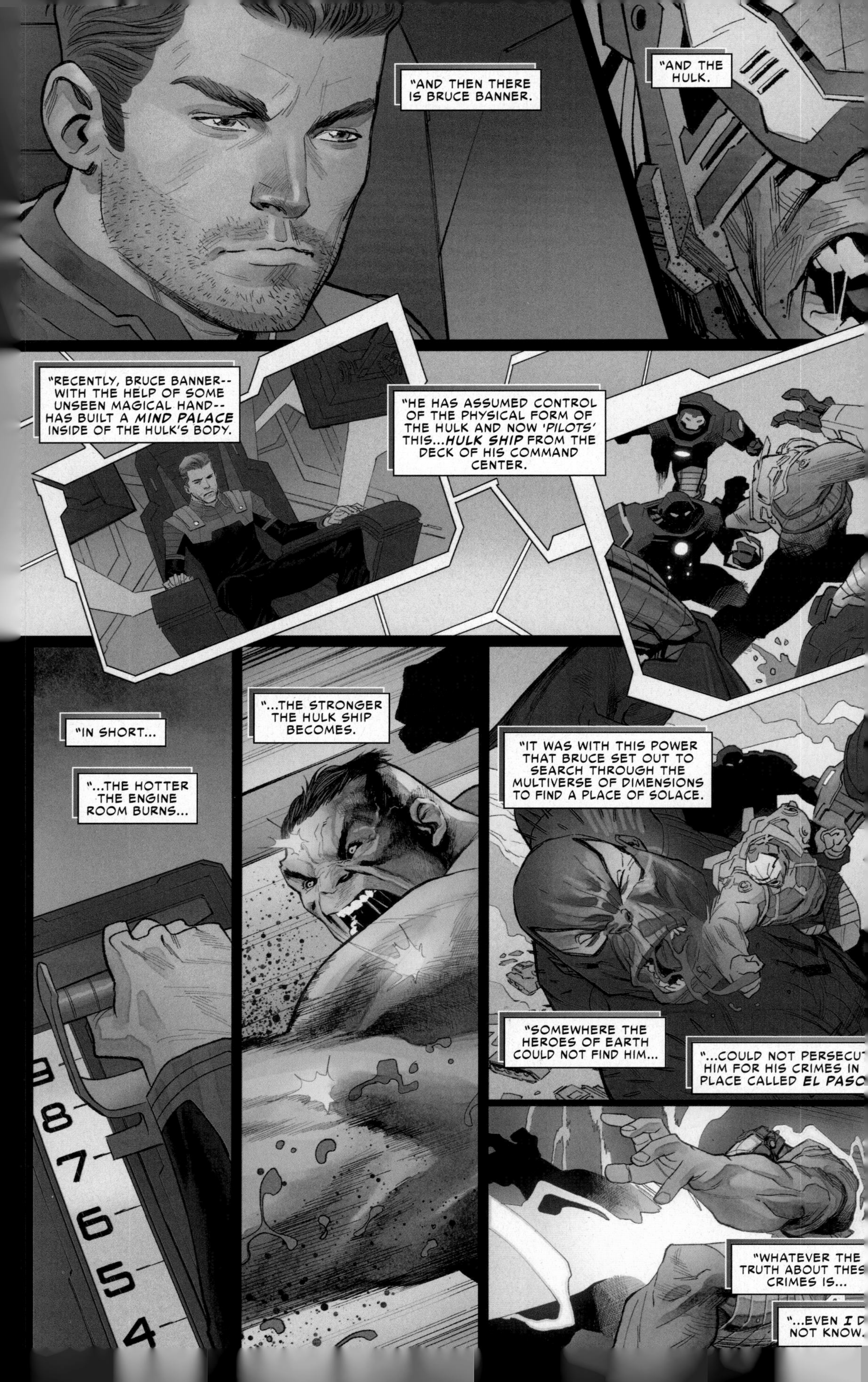
"AND THEN THERE IS BRUCE BANNER.
"AND THE HULK.
"RECENTLY, BRUCE BANNER--WITH THE HELP OF SOME UNSEEN MAGICAL HAND--HAS BUILT A MIND PALACE INSIDE OF THE HULK'S BODY.
"HE HAS ASSUMED CONTROL OF THE PHYSICAL FORM OF THE HULK AND NOW 'PILOTS' THIS...HULK SHIP FROM THE DECK OF HIS COMMAND CENTER.
"IN SHORT...
"...THE HOTTER THE ENGINE ROOM BURNS...
"...THE STRONGER THE HULK SHIP BECOMES.
"IT WAS WITH THIS POWER THAT BRUCE SET OUT TO SEARCH THROUGH THE MULTIVERSE OF DIMENSIONS TO FIND A PLACE OF SOLACE.
"SOMEWHERE THE HEROES OF EARTH COULD NOT FIND HIM...
"...COULD NOT PERSECUT HIM FOR HIS CRIMES IN PLACE CALLED EL PASO
"WHATEVER THE TRUTH ABOUT THES CRIMES IS...
"...EVEN I D NOT KNOW.
9 8 7 6 5 4

"AND THE ENGINE ROOM.
"THE SHIP ITSELF IS POWERED BY THE HULK'S OWN PERSONA...
"...TRAPPED IN THE 'ENGINE ROOM' AND TORTURED BY A SERIES OF NEVER-ENDING AND ALWAYS-GROWING ADVERSARIES.
"BUT PERHAPS WE SHALL SOON FIND OUT...
"...BECAUSE...IN THIS VERY MOMENT...
"...AGAINST A BATTLEGROUND OF STRANGE AND UNSEEN WORLDS...
"...ROARING ACROSS THE IN-BETWEEN SPACES OF REALITY...
"...IT IS HERE...

"...THAT OUR STORIES COLLIDE."
STOP THIS, BANNER!
I KNOW YOU CAN HEAR ME! SOMEWHERE DEEP INSIDE!
CONTROL YOUR RAGE AND--
THOR.
SHUT UP.
WHUMP

GAKK-REEN.
"A WRETCHED PLANET FILLED WITH DISEASE-PLAGUED, WAR MONGERING CANNIBALS THAT DEVOUR THE EYES OF THEIR YOUNG TO APPEASE THEIR ALL-KNOWING PAIN GOD.
"IT SMELLS OF COTTON CANDY. AND PUPPY PAWS. AND THE PAIN GOD IS ALWAYS HAPPY."
BOOOM
BOOOOM
I CAN HEAR YOU JUST FINE.

GET UP, BOY! IF THE APE WANTS A BATTLE, THEN LET'S--
WILL YOU LET ME HANDLE THIS, FATHER?
HE'S CLOSING IN!
I NEED A FULL SYSTEM AND ENGINE CHECK.
COMPUTER, RUN A DIAGNOSTIC ON HULL INTEGRITY BEFORE WE--
THIS ISN'T GOING TO BE LIKE THE OTHER FIGHTS, BRUCE.
DAMMIT, BOY, JUST LISTEN TO ME! LET ME LOOSE AND I'LL--
THERE ARE INNOCENT CREATURES ON THIS PLANET! I WILL NOT ALLOW YOU TO WAGE ALL-OUT WAR UNTIL--
OH, GROW UP AND GET TO WORK, SON! THIS PLANET WILL--
NAY, DAMN YOU! SIF WILL FIND US A SUITABLE PLACE FOR COMBAT AND--
YOU'VE DONE THIS BEFORE. DO YOU REALLY THINK YOU CAN BEAT HIM THIS TIME? AFTER EVERYTHING THAT--
ENOUGH, "BETTY"! JUS
--LEAVE ME ALONE!!!
--THAT IS FINAL!

WHO ARE YOU TALKING TO?
WHO ARE YOU TALKING TO?
AGHHH!!
AYE! THAT'S MORE LIKE IT!

OKAY. LET'S DO THIS.
KLK
BANNER!!!
I AWAIT YOUR ORDERS, THOR. GIVE ME A PLACE. ANYWHERE!
WHAT ARE YOU WAITING FOR, BOY?! LET'S TEAR THIS EMERALD IDIOT INTO--
SIF!!! ANYWHERE. SOMEWHERE CAN DO BAT SAFELY!!!
BUT DO IT NOW!!!
UM...
...OKAY...
WOOOOM

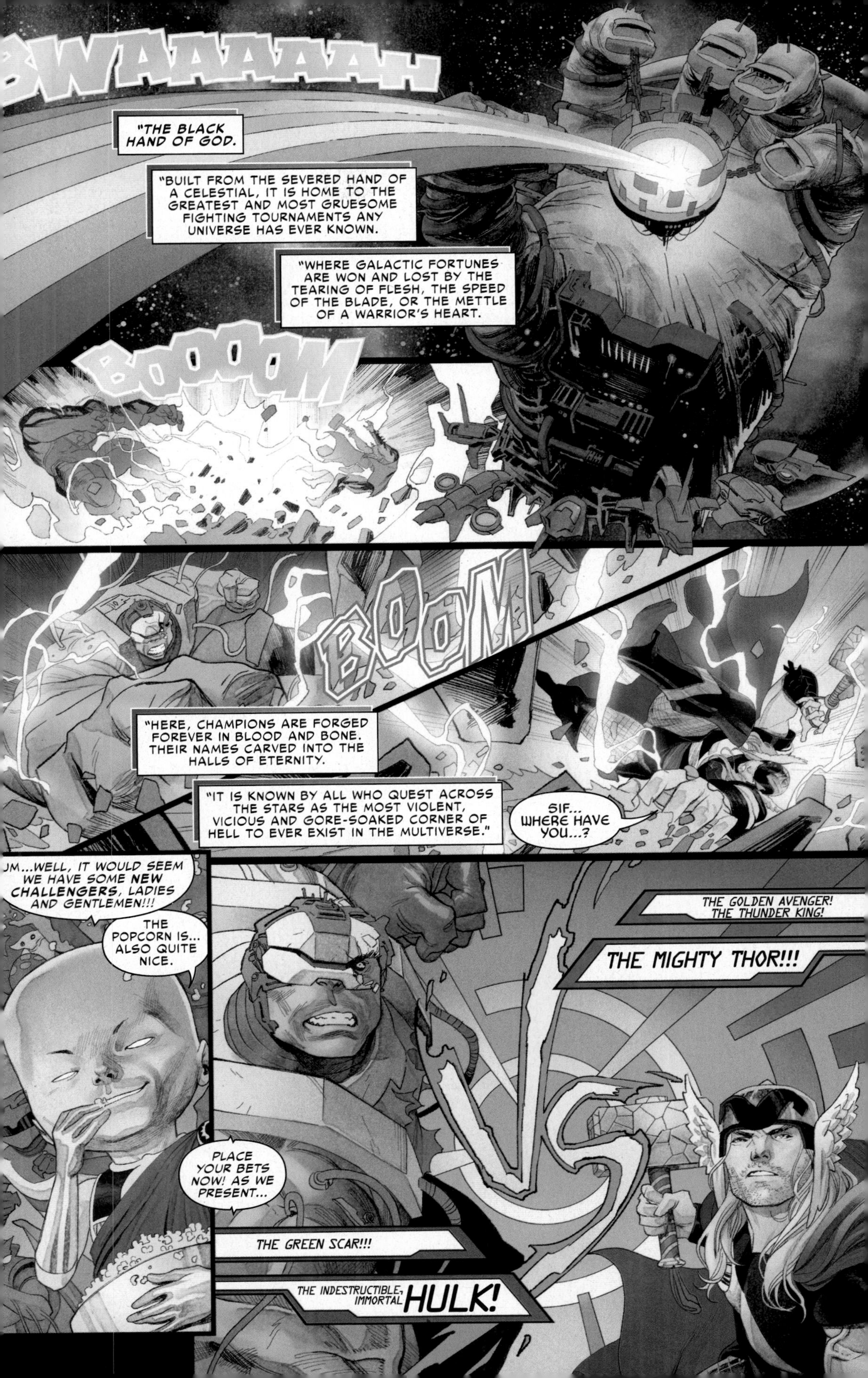
BWAAAAAAH
"THE BLACK HAND OF GOD.
"BUILT FROM THE SEVERED HAND OF A CELESTIAL, IT IS HOME TO THE GREATEST AND MOST GRUESOME FIGHTING TOURNAMENTS ANY UNIVERSE HAS EVER KNOWN.
"WHERE GALACTIC FORTUNES ARE WON AND LOST BY THE TEARING OF FLESH, THE SPEED OF THE BLADE, OR THE METTLE OF A WARRIOR'S HEART.
BOOOOM
BOOM
"HERE, CHAMPIONS ARE FORGED FOREVER IN BLOOD AND BONE. THEIR NAMES CARVED INTO THE HALLS OF ETERNITY.
"IT IS KNOWN BY ALL WHO QUEST ACROSS THE STARS AS THE MOST VIOLENT, VICIOUS AND GORE-SOAKED CORNER OF HELL TO EVER EXIST IN THE MULTIVERSE."
SIF... WHERE HAVE YOU...?
JM...WELL, IT WOULD SEEM WE HAVE SOME NEW CHALLENGERS, LADIES AND GENTLEMEN!!!
THE POPCORN IS... ALSO QUITE NICE.
THE GOLDEN AVENGER! THE THUNDER KING!
THE MIGHTY THOR!!!
PLACE YOUR BETS NOW! AS WE PRESENT...
THE GREEN SCAR!!!
THE INDESTRUCTIBLE, IMMORTAL HULK!

HULK

THOR
ROUND ONE!
FIGHT!

THOR! LISTEN TO ME! YOU CAN'T--
SEVENTEEN!!!
BOOOOM
SEVENTEEN? WHAT...WHAT ARE YOU TALKING ABOUT?
HAVE YOU FORGOTTEN ALREADY?!
IS KILLING THIS EASY FOR YOU NOW?
SEVENTEEN, BRUCE.
BOOOM

CHUNK
AGHH!!!
RRR... GET...YOUR HAMMER...
SEVENTEEN PEOPLE DEAD IN EL PASO.
SEVENTEEN DEAD BECAUSE OF YOU.
I AM SORRY, BRUCE. BUT I BELIEVE YOU AND I BOTH KNOW IT WAS ALWAYS GOING TO END THIS WAY.
ONE CAN ONLY CAGE A MONSTER FOR SO LONG.
AND SO THIS FALLS TO ME, OLD FRIEND. I'M AFRAID THIS IS GOODBYE. IF IT EASES YOU...I WILL NOT REVEL IN THIS VICTORY. I WILL ALWAYS KNOW YOU AS--
RAAAGHHH!!! THAT WASN'T ME!!!
THOR! PLEASE! LET ME UP AND I CAN--
PLEASE. STOP. MJOLNIR WILL NOT BE MOVED. AND NEITHER SHALL I.
RAAGHHHH!!!

COMPUTER, INCREASE ENGINE ROOM TO LEVEL EIGHT AND HOLD.
BUT SIR. WE ARE PINNED DOWN BY THE HAMMER OF THOR. IT CANNOT BE MOVED. NO MATTER HOW STRONG OR ANGRY WE--
HOW DO YOU KNOW THAT?
...YOUR MEMORY FILES, SIR. I HAVE ACCESS TO EVERY FIGHT THAT YOU HAVE--
EXACTLY. GIVE ME FULL HAPTICS. SLAVE CONTROLS TO ME.
I'M GOING IN.
SIR, I HIGHLY RECOMMEND AGAINST THIS COURSE OF ACTION.
NOTED. WE'VE FOUGHT HIM AND BEAT HIM BEFORE.

I'M NOT SCARED.
SIR, IF I MAY... THE HULK HAS FOUGHT HIM.
NOT YOU.
EXACTLY.
WE'VE FOUGHT HARDER...
...LET'S FIGHT SMARTER.
RUN DIAGNOSTICS. I NEED DATA. I NEED EVERY FIGHT.
SIR?
YOU SAID YOU HAVE ACCESS TO EVERY FIGHT WE'VE EVER HAD, RIGHT? EVERY TIME THE HULK HAS CLASHED WITH THOR?
FILES FOUND, SIR. ARE YOU SURE ABOUT--?
GIVE IT TO ME. I WANT TO FEEL IT.
EVERY PUNCH. EVERY BATTLE. I WANT TO FEEL IT!
DO IT!!! DO IT RIGHT N--

RAAGGHHH!!

RAAGGHHH!!
no...
GODS...
UGHH... HGHHH...
RHHGGHPPP

THOR.
PICK UP YOUR HAMMER.
AYE.
NOW.
WHERE WERE WE?

OH YEAH...
HULK!
T UP, HAT ARE OING?!
I'M-- TRYING, DAMN YOU!
FINE. MUST I DO EVERYTHING?!

SMASH!!!
AGHH!
VOOOOMMMM
TRYING WHAT?
TRYING TO BREATHE? TO MOVE?
SORRY, THOR. I TRIED TO REASON WITH YOU. I DID.
BUT YOU ARE NOT GOING TO TAKE ME IN. I'M SORRY, I AM, BUT THIS IS WHERE THIS--
...ENDS?
BOOM

RMMMBBBLL
HA! IS THAT RAIN?! YOU THINK YOUR THUNDERSTORMS ARE GOING TO HURT ME?!
NOT... THUNDER...
WHAT?
THAT WAS MJOLNIR...
...BREAKING THE SOUND BARRIER.
...
WHAT?

KRAAABOOOOM

THOR, LISTEN TO ME. WHEN I STRUCK HULK, I...FELT SOMETHING. SOMETHING IS--
--WRONG. YES, I FEEL IT AS WELL. IT'S AS IF HE'S POSSESSED...
NOT POSSESSED. NO...
"...HAUNTED."
UGGHH...
LET ME LOOSE, SON. I HAVE AN IDEA...
AYE.
BOOOM
BANNER! IF YOU WILL NOT RELENT--IF YOU WILL NOT LISTEN TO REASON...
BOOOM

...THEN
ERHAPS YOU
VILL LISTEN
TO THIS!
EVASIVE
ANEUVERS! NOW!
NOW! N--
BOOOOOOM
AGHH!!!
BOOM
BRUCE BANNER...
NO...

...I WOULD HAVE WORDS WITH THEE.

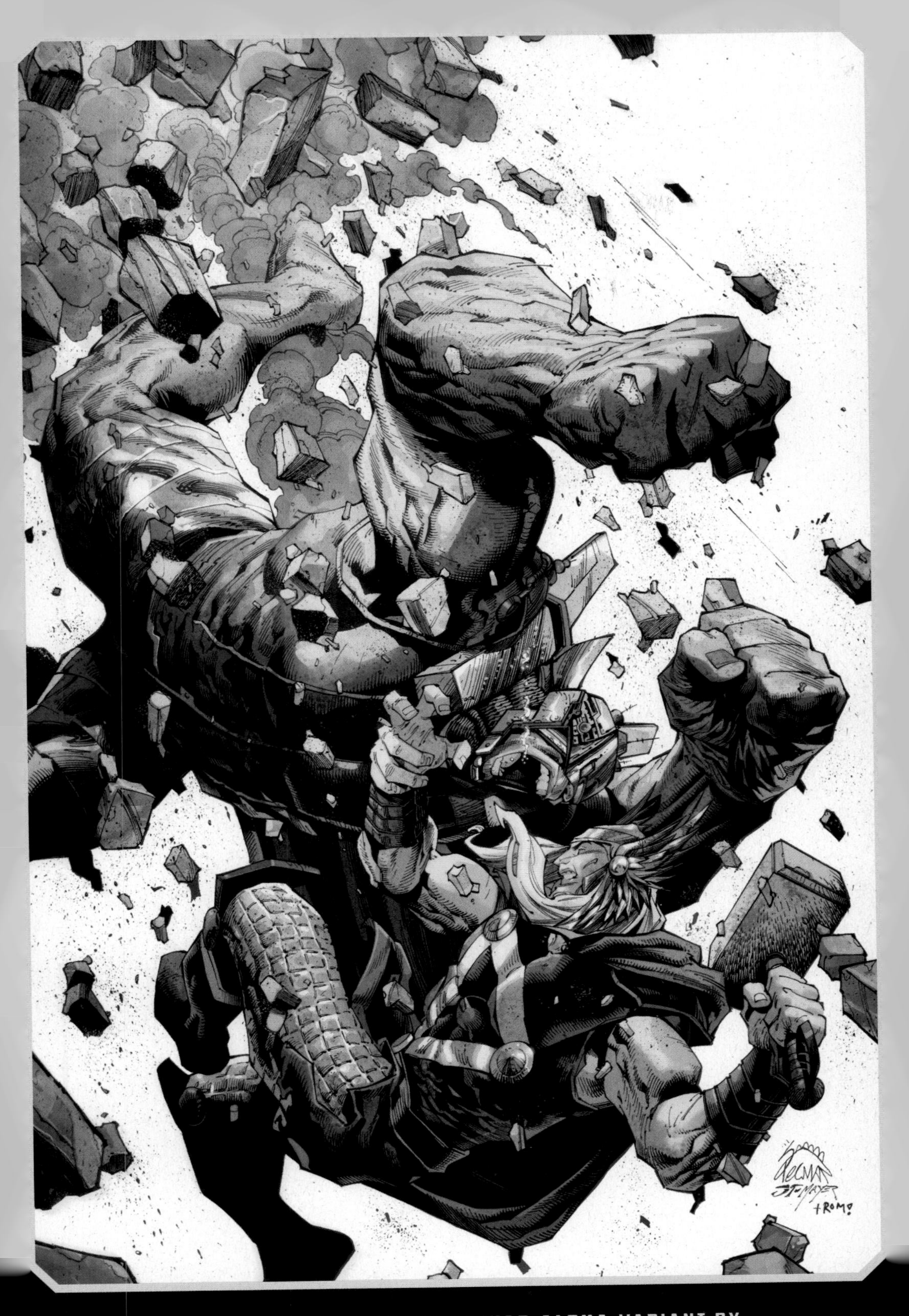

HULK VS. THOR: BANNER OF WAR ALPHA VARIANT BY

RYAN STEGMAN, JP MAYER & ROMULO FAJARDO JR.

THOR #25
BANNER OF WAR PART TWO

ENGERS MOUNTAIN.
WE FOUND HIM.

THIS IS...
WHAT IS THIS?
IT'S AN ARENA. LOCALS CALL IT THE BLACK HAND OF GOD. A SEVERED HAND OF A CELESTIAL RETROFITTED FOR INTERGALACTIC BLOOD SPORT AND BURIED IN THE DEEPEST REACHES OF UNCHARTED SPACE.
THAT... THAT IS--
YEAH...
...IT'S AWESOME.
I WAS GOING TO SAY TERRIFYING.
BUT HOW CAN YOU BE SURE HE'S THERE? HOW DID YOU FIND THIS PLACE?
I HAVE A NETWORK OF DEEP SPACE SATELLITES SLAVED TO MY INTERNAL MAINFRAME. THEY CONSTANTLY SWEEP FOR ACTIVITY IN PLACES EXPLORED OR NOT.
YESTERDAY, WE PICKED UP A SOUND.
A SOUND? IN--
YES. A SOUND. IN SPACE. SOMETHING SO LOUD THAT ITS VIBRATIONAL FREQUENCY COMPLETELY FRIED ONE OF MY SPACE BABIES.
FROM THERE, I TRIANGULATED THE SOURCE OF THE SONIC DISTURBANCE AND ISOLATED IT.
YOU KNOW WHAT IT WAS?
IT WAS A VOICE, REED. A VOICE SO LOUD THAT IT BLEW A SATELLITE OUT OF THE SKY FROM TWO THOUSAND MILES AWAY.
IT SAID "HULK. SMASH."

WELL...THAT IS... IMPRESSIVE, TONY. NO SRESPECT INTENDED, BUT I HAD NO IDEA YOU HAD OSE KINDS OF RESOURCES FRANKLY, THE SCIENTIFIC NOW-HOW TO SWEEP THE DEPTHS OF UNKNOWN SPACE LIKE THAT. AND THEN TO--
I'M KIDDING, REED. I HAVE NO IDEA HOW TO DO ANY OF THAT.
THOR'S RAVENS TOLD ME WHERE HULK IS.
RAVENS? WHAT...?
...
HUH?
OKAY, LISTEN. WE KNOW WHERE HE IS.
IF THOR IS ALREADY ENGAGED WITH BANNER, I SAY WE HANG TIGHT UNTIL WE HAVE MORE INTEL.
MM-HMM. YEAH.
NO, I'M GONNA GO FIGHT HIM.
STEVE IS RIGHT. IF THE EVENTS OF EL PASO HAVE TAUGHT US ANYTHING...IT'S THAT IT'S TIME WE STOPPED LYING TO OURSELVES ABOUT WHAT BRUCE IS CAPABLE OF.

ABSOLUTELY NOT.
I AM TELLING YOU TO STAND DOWN!
I WASN'T ASKING FOR PERMISSION.
YOU'RE NOT UNDERSTANDING ME, CAP.
HULK. BRUCE... WHATEVER THE HELL HE IS NOW...
I LOOKED INTO HIS EYES WHEN HE--
--INITIATE THRUSTER SEQUENCE--
--WHEN HE ATTACKED ME IN WUNDAGORE.*
*SEE HULK #1. --WIL
HE WAS GOING TO KILL ME.
HE TRIED...TO KILL ME.
AND, WELL...I GOTTA TELL YA, CAP: I DIDN'T CARE FOR IT.
SO...ONCE AGAIN--
THRUSTERS AT FULL CAPACITY AND HOLDING.
--STAND BY FOR LAUNCH COMMAND--
--I'M GONNA GO KICK HIS ASS.
AND I HAVE A NICE NEW TOY I'VE BEEN WORKING ON THAT WILL--
I'M NEVER AT THESE MEETINGS, CAP.
WAIT. ARE YOU HERE?
I HAVE PLACES TO BE.
LAUNCH

THREE.
SEE YOU ON THE OTHER SIDE, CAP.
TWO.
TONY!!!
ONE.
KRAKKA-DOOOOM

KRAK
AGH!!!
STARSHIP HULK COMMAND DECK.
I AM NO MAN OF SCIENCE, BRUCE BANNER.
BUT I AM WILLING TO WAGER THAT KILLING Y WILL BRING TH MONSTER DOW AS WELL.
I DO NOT WISH THIS TO COME TO THAT.
BUT I WILL IF I MUST.
YOU'RE NOT A MAN AT ALL, ODIN.
YOU'RE A GHOST.
THHP
THHP
AND YOU'RE IN MY HOUSE.

...BANNER?
RAGH!!! DAMN YOU!!!
DID YOU REALLY THINK YOU COULD WALK IN HERE?
THAT I WOULD BE AFRAID OF YOU?
...ARE YOU...IN THERE?
YOU MAY BE POWERFUL, OLD MAN.
BUT IN HERE...
...I'M GOD.

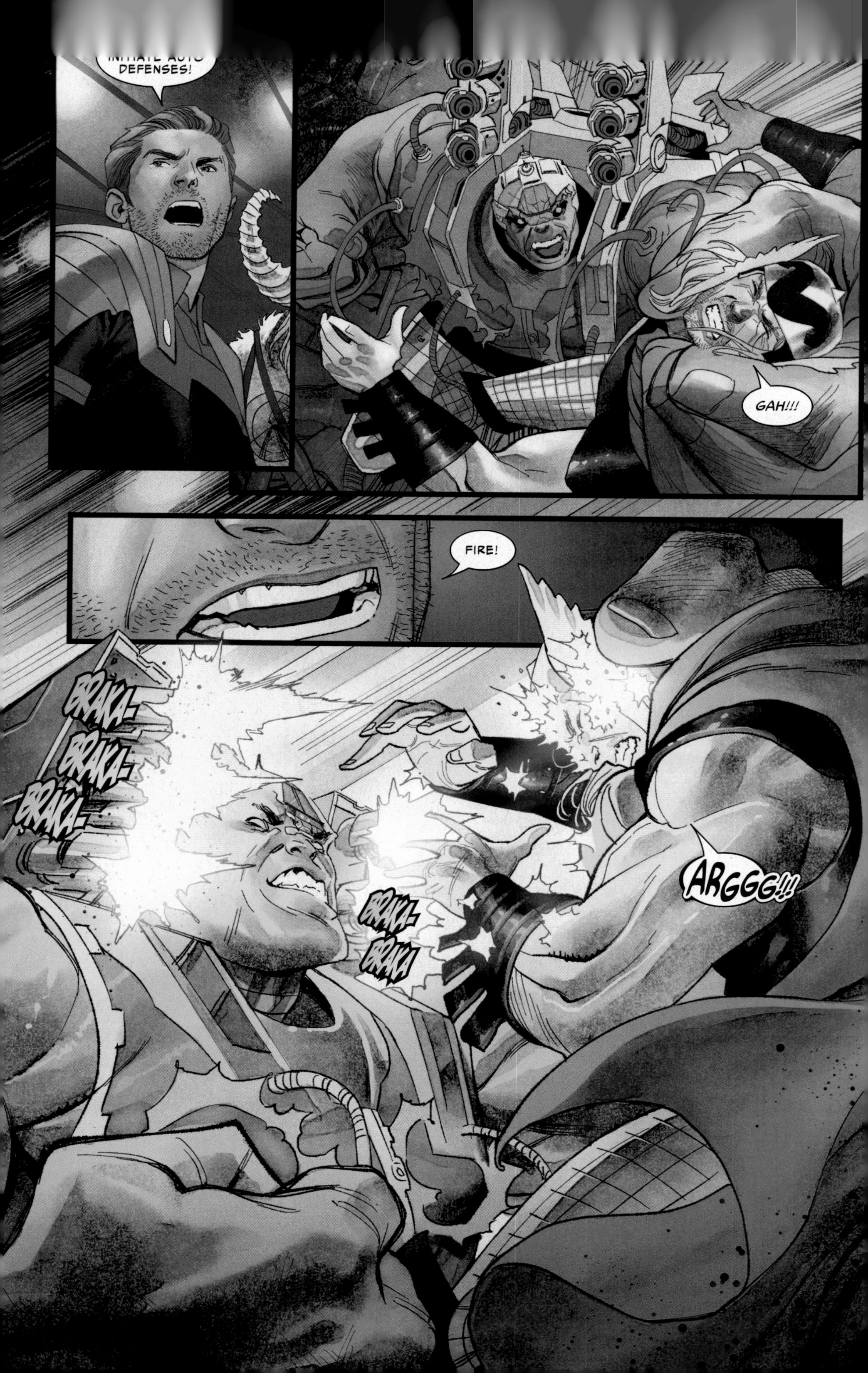
DEFENSES!
GAH!!!
FIRE!
BRAKA-
BRAKA-
BRAKA-
BRAKA-
BRAKA
ARGGG!!!

THERE. NOW LET'S YOU AND I--
OOOM
HUU!!!
AGGHH!!!
WAIT. WAIT...NO... JUST HAVE TO--
HKK--
NOT BAD FOR A GHOST, EH, BOY?

THAT!
IS!!
ENOUGH!!!
BOOOOOM
AGH!

BANNER, WAKE UP!
WHAT IN THE HEL HAVE YOU DONE?! WHERE AM I?
WH-WHAT IS HAPPENING?
YOU TELL ME.
WE'RE IN YOUR HEAD, DOCTOR.
OH.
OH GOD. NO...

WE'RE IN EL PASO.
THIS...
...THIS IS WHERE IT HAPPENED.
I...I CAN'T BE HERE. WHY IS THIS HAPPENING? I LOCKED THIS AWAY! I DON'T WANT TO SEE THIS AGAIN! I DON'T...
YOUR DEFENSES ARE DOWN. YOUR MIND IS EXPOSED. AND THIS IS WHERE IT'S TAKEN US.
WHAT HAPPENED HERE, BANNER? WHY ARE YOU SO AFRAID?
IT WASN'T.. IT WASN'T SUPPOSED T BE LIKE THIS...
THE HULK...
...WE FACED DOWN THE DEVIL AND WALKED AWAY. WE SURVIVED.
WE... FORGAVE EACH OTHER.
DECIDED TO SEE THE WORLD IN A NEW WAY.
TO SAVE THE WORLD.
TOGETHER.

D THEN
E CAME
HERE.
THERE HAD BEEN REPORTS OF SOMETHING KILLING PEOPLE ALONG THE BORDER. PEOPLE WHO...
...WHO JUST WANTED A BETTER LIFE.
SO IT FOUND YOU? IS THAT IT? IT CAME HERE, AND YOU--
NO.
THE MONSTER NEVER SHOWED.
AGH!
HEY!
AH, SORRY, PAL.
BUT SOMETHING ELSE DID.
I COULD FEEL IT...
HULK'S RAGE INSIDE OF ME...
...BOILING.
HGH!
I'M--I'M SORRY. QUICK TEMPER, HAHA. HEY, WHY DON'T YOU LET ME BUY YOU ANOTHER--
IT--I DON'T KNOW HOW TO DESCRIBE IT. IT WAS DIFFERENT. LIKE IT WAS...
...COMING OFF OF ME. LIKE I WAS... CONTAGIOUS.
OH MAN! YOUR SKIN! YOU'RE BURNING UP! YOU'RE--

PUNY BANNER!
WHA--? NO!!! NO, YOU CAN'T--
AGHH!!!
AND THEN IT SPREAD.
ALL OF THEM. *INFECTED.*
BY RAGE.

BY ME.
BY *HIM*.
WHEN I OPENED MY EYES AGAIN... WHEN I COULD MOVE--
--I SAW *BLACK*.
DEAD
THERE WAS SOMETHING ELSE IN THE DRIVER'S SEAT.
SOMETHING NEW.
SOMETHING *HORRIFYING*.
AND I...

"...I WAS HELPLESS.
"LOCKED INSIDE OF MY OWN BODY.
"UNABLE TO STOP.
"POWERLESS AS THIS THING...
"I WASN'T ALLOWED TO EVEN BLINK AS IT USED MY BODY AS A WEAPON.
"I COULD SCREAM.
"I COULD FEEL TEARS WET ON MY CHEEKS.

"...RIPPED EVERYONE IN THE ROOM TO PIECES.
"IT WOULDN'T STOP. IT COULDN'T BE STOPPED.
"AND...AND IT MADE ME WATCH.
"I COULD HEAR MYSELF TELLING THESE MEN TO RUN.
"THAT I WAS SORRY.
"BUT NO ONE COULD HEAR ME OVER THE SOUNDS OF ROARING AND BREAKING BONES.
"AND THEN... SUDDENLY..."

...IT WAS OVER.
I STOOD THERE ALL NIGHT, WATCHING THE FIRE.
WISHING THAT I WAS INSIDE OF IT.
HOPING THAT SOMEONE WOULD COME. TO SAVE ME...
...TO *KILL* ME.
BUT THEY NEVER DID.
SO THAT'S WHEN I DECIDED. IF THAT FURY THAT'S INSIDE OF ME CANNOT BE TAMED--CANNOT BE FORGIVEN OR MENDED--
--EVEN AFTER BEATING THE DEVIL...
...THEN I WOULD *USE* IT. LIKE HE USED ME.
GODS...BUT HOW? HOW DID YOU BUILD ALL OF THIS? THERE ARE GREAT MAGICS AT WORK HERE. HOW DID YOU--
RMMMMMMBBLL
WHAT IS THIS? WHAT'S GOING ON?!
THOR! NO, DAMN YOU! NOT YET! NOT--
AGHH!!!

WWWSHS
FWWAP
DAMN YOU, BOY! I NEED MORE TIME. SEND ME BACK!
THAT'S JUST IT, FATHER.
WE DON'T HAVE ANY MORE TIME.
WHAT THE HEL S THAT?
THE CAVALRY.
OH GOD. OH GOD. NO...
PLEASE! COME BACK! YOU DON'T UNDERSTAND! HE DOESN'T KNOW!
"HE DOESN'T KNOW HE'S NOT IN A SIMULATION!!!"
HEY BRUCE. LONG TIME NO SMASH.
SORRY TO HAVE TO DO THIS, BIG GUY...

...BUT I'M GONNA HAVE TO ASK YOU TO STEP OUT OF THE VEHICLE.

THOR #25 VARIANT BY

JOHN ROMITA JR., KLAUS JANSON & JASON KEITH

HULK #7
BANNER OF WAR PART THREE

LIGHTS BURN THE SKY IN HIS MIND.
AND THOUGH IT IS A MIND ACCUSTOMED TO THE FIRE...
...TO THE RAGE...
...HE YET WEEPS.
I'M SO SORRY...
FOR MORE THAN MOST EVER HAVE...
...AND FEW ELSE EVER WILL...
...BRUCE BANNER KNOWS WHAT THE FIRE BRINGS.
...FOR WHAT YOU'VE UNLEASHED.

HE KNOWS WHAT THE RAGE AWAKENS.

ARRRRRGGH!

THE BLACK HAND OF GOD LAYS EMPTY FOR THE FIRST TIME IN MILLENNIA.
ITS KNUCKLES UNCLENCHED AS THE POWER OF A CELESTIAL SUN SCORCHES ITS PALM.
THE LAST REMAINING JACKALS AND MORBIDLY CURIOUS GHOULS OF THIS QUADRANT SQUABBLE AND COLLECT THEIR UNEARNED WINNINGS AS THE BIFROST SCATTERS THEM TO THE WINDS.
WHAT COMES NEXT WILL HAVE NO WITNESSES. NO WATCHERS.
NONE SAVE THOR.
THE VOICE OF HIS DEAD FATHER RINGING IN HIS EAR...
...AND THE SMELL OF BURNING FLESH. ANCIENT, CELESTIAL, AND LONG DEAD...
AND BEHIND IT, THE ROARING OF MUSCLE AND SINEW.
BURNING AND GROWING, YET STILL UNDER THE HEA
OF A COSMIC MAELSTRO
...WHICH UNLEASHES AN INFINITE OCEAN OF PAIN THAT HUMANKIND CANNOT PERCEIVE...
...UPON A CREATURE THAT KNOWS NOT WHY IT MUST SUFFER.

REATURE...
BORN.
SET FREE FROM A CAGE MADE FROM HIS REFLECTION.
UM... B.O.S.S.? WHAT'S GOING ON?
IT WASN'T EASY TURNING THIS CELESTIAL'S BODY INTO HULKBUSTER ARMOR THAT COULD DRAIN THE GAMMA RADIATION OUT OF HULK SO WE COULD SAFELY APPREHEND HIM. DON'T GET ME WRONG, IT'S DOING ITS JOB...
...BUT A) THIS IS AN INSANE AMOUNT OF GAMMA, AND B) HOW IS HE STILL STANDING? SHOULDN'T HE BE...YOU KNOW, SMALLER?
INCORRECT. POWER LEVELS SURGING. GAMMA RADIATION INCREASING.
WHAT?? FROM WHERE?!
FROM HIS SHADOW.
FROM THE ONLY MAN HE KNEW AS FRIEND.
ONLY TO FACE THE WRATH OF A GOD.
AND THE CELESTIAL JUDGMENT OF A HUNDRED THOUSAND EXPLODING STARS.
IT IS TOO MUCH.
IT IS TOO MUCH.

IT IS TOO MUCH.
AGGHH!!! FALL DOWN, DAMN YOU!
IT IS...
...TOO MUCH.
IT IS...
TOOOOO

...TOO MUCH.
DOOOOOOOOOMM
ALERT. CRITICAL DAMAGE TO INTERNAL SYSTEMS.
→COUGH← YEAH! YEAH, I FELT THAT! THANKS!
WHAT THE HELL WAS THAT? HOW IS BANNER *THAT* STRONG? IS THAT EVEN POSS--
YOU HAVE SUSTAINED MULTIPLE BROKEN RIBS AND A FRACTURED COLLARBONE. INITIATING CELESTIAL SELF-HEALING PROTOCOLS AND DIAGNOSTICS.
IT IS...
ADMINISTERING SEDATIVE AND SLAVING CONTROLS TO--
NO! NO. GET ME UP. I NEED TO--
...WAIT. WHAT THE...?

...ENOUGH.
TONY...
IF YOU CAN HEAR ME IN THERE... STAY DOWN.

UH. HEY, BUD.
IT'S ME. IRON MAN.
OF THE AVENGERS? THE TEAM YOU'RE ON? YOU...YOU CALLED ME HERE?? NOW YOU TRY TO KILL ME? WHAT THE HELL, MAN?!
I APOLOGIZE, OLD FRIEND. THAT WAS...NOT OF MY OWN DOING.
MY...HAMMER... IT...REACTED... POORLY. IT IS STUBBORN AND OLD AND...INCREASINGLY DEFIANT.
I'M SORRY. YOU...YOUR HAMMER??
HOW MANY TIMES ARE WE GOING TO SING THIS SONG, THOR?
I THOUGHT YOU KILLED THE BIG, BLUE LIGHTNING LADY THAT WAS MAKING YOUR HAMMER EVIL--DIDN'T WE JUST DO THAT?
GOTTA SAY, THIS ISN'T GOING TO LOOK GOOD ON THE QUARTERLIES, BIG GUY.
JUST TELL HIM, DAMMIT! MAYBE HE'LL LISTEN TO ME!
HULK IS NOT IN CONTROL!
I KNOW THAT!
TONY...I KNOW THAT. YES. I'VE BEEN...ERRATIC, BUT YOU MUST TRUST ME. THERE IS MORE AT PLAY HERE THAN EITHER OF US KNOW. WE HAVE NEVER FACED ANYTHING LIKE THIS BEFORE.
I FEAR WE MAY HAVE TO TAKE BANNER DOWN FOR GOOD THIS--
FOR BURI'S SAKE, SON! BEHIND YOU!

BOOOM
BANNER!!!
OH, I DON'T KNOW...
...SEEMS LIKE GOOD OL' HULK TO ME.
NO!!!

BOOOM
BOOM
YOU DON'T UNDERSTAND!
"HE DOESN'T KNOW!
"HE DOESN'T KNOW HE'S NOT IN A SIMULATION ANYMORE! HE DOESN'T UNDERSTAND THAT YOU'RE BOTH REAL! THAT HE CAN KILL YOU!!!
"HE'S NOT GOING TO OLD BACK!"
RNGGHGH...
ROUND TWO, BIG GUY.

LET'S GO!!!
RAGGHHH!!!
RAGHHHH! BANNER!!!
THOR?! LITTLE HELP?!
BOOM

WHAT ARE YOU--
YOU DON'T LISTEN, BOY! HE NEEDS OUR HELP!
WHO?! WHAT ARE YOU--
DAMN YOU! LET ME--
FATHER!
--GO!!!
HULK...
FATHER, NO!!!
...WORTHY?

BOOOOM
CALM DOWN, FRIEND. EVERYTHING IS ALL RIGHT...
I'M NOT HERE FOR *YOU.*
RNGHH!
I'M HERE TO SEE **DOCT**
BANNER.
BANNER!!!

RAGHHH!!!
FWAASSHHH
WHOA!
BOOOOM
--THE HELL WAS THAT?? HULK CAN SHOOT EYE LASERS NOW?! THOR, WHAT ARE YOU SEEING?
MJOLNIR HAS HIM PINNED. BUT HE IS...UNRELENTING... UNLEASHED.
HIS RAGE... IT BURNS THE VERY GROUND BELOW HIM. I HAVE NEVER SEEN THIS BEFORE...
LET!
WHOA. I'M GETTING SOME READINGS HERE. THAT'S NOT RAGE BURNING THE GROUND OUT THERE.
THAT'S GAMMA. A WHOLE HELL OF A LOT OF IT. LIKE... "MELT AN ENTIRE CITY SKYLINE" LEVELS.
THOR, YOU AVE TO GET T OF THERE! NOW!!!
FATHER!!! TO ME!! WE MUST--
NAY!! I CAN REACH HIM!
HULK!!
I CAN--
FREE!!!

GAH!
WHA--?
OH...OH GOD...

DID...
DID WE KNOW HE COULD DO THAT?
THOR? YOU THERE?
B.O.S.S., TALK TO ME... TELL ME I'M NOT TRAPPED ALONE WITHOUT A BATTLE BOT ON A DYING PLANET WITH A SUPER HULK...
THE CELESTIAL TECH SHIELDED YOU FROM THE GAMMA IRRADIATION RESULTING FROM THE GAMMA BOMB.
THAT WASN'T A GAMMA BOMB!
TO BE PRECISE...IT WAS APPROXIMATELY THE FORCE OF THREE THOUSAND GAMMA BOMBS, SIR.
OH. GOODIE. UM... HYPOTHETICAL...
...IF SOMEONE...SAY, HUMAN... WAS CAUGHT IN THAT BLAST... LIKE BANNER WAS. WOULD THAT--?
CREATE A HULK? NO, SIR. IT WOULD ATOMIZE THEM.
GREAT... AND, UM...JUST FOR GIGGLES...
...WHAT IF THEY WEREN'T HUMAN?

"WHAT IF THEY WERE A *GOD?*"
THOR...
...SMASH!!!

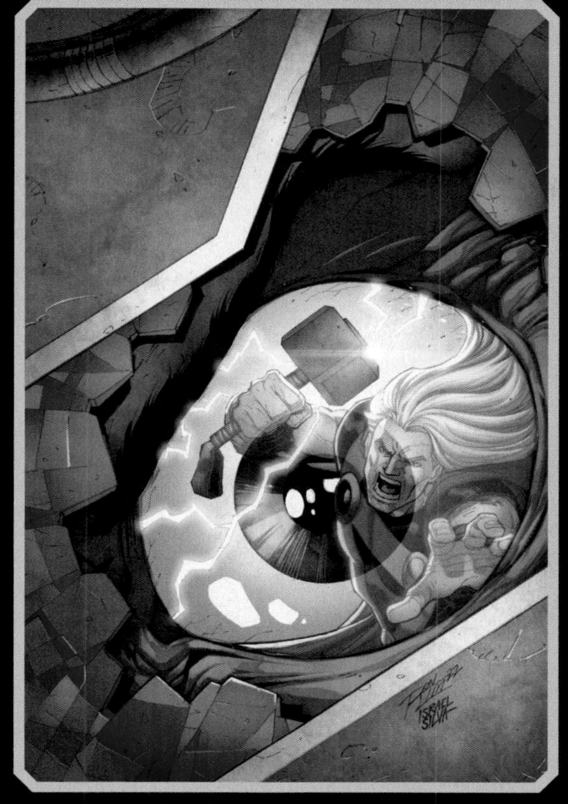

THOR #25 VARIANT BY **RON LIM & ISRAEL SILVA**

THOR #25 VARIANT BY **CHRISSIE ZULLO**

HULK #7 VARIANT BY **CHRISSIE ZULLO**

THOR #26
BANNER OF WAR PART FOUR
ANDERSON

D THEN...THERE AS NOTHING.
NOTHING LEFT...
...BUT RAGE.
THOR...

RAGE IN THE THUNDER.
SMASH!!!
THOR!!!

RAGHH!!!
BWAAHH
AGHH!!!
VKSHH
STOP! THIS ISN'T YOU!!!
PLEASE... DON'T MAKE ME--
RAGHHH!!!

KRAK
BOOM
BOOOM
HMMPF...
...
...BRUCE?
...
NO.
NO BRUCE.

YOU...
...RUN.
BOOOM
RAGHHH!!!
AGHHHHH!!!

KRAKKAA-DOOOOOM

AGH!!!
DEAR...DEAR GOD, WHAT IS HAPPENING OUT THERE?
THOR.
HE'S
LING YOU,
ANNER.
YOU
URNED HIM INTO A MONSTER. LIKE YOU.
LIKE... WHATEVER THE HEL YOU ARE...
AND NOW YOU'RE GOING TO GET UP AND STOP BEING SO DAMNED WEAK AND HELP ME BEAT SOME SENSE BACK INTO HIM.
YOU'RE
AMN RIGHT I AM.
WHAT DO YOU NEED?
I HAVE TO GET BACK INTO MY CONTROL CENTER--HULK HAS TAKEN OVER AS THE PRIME PERSONALITY DRIVING THE SHIP.
I HAVE TO TAKE IT BACK.
AYE. IF YOU UNDERSTAND WHAT YOU JUST SAID, THAT IS GOOD ENOUGH FOR ME. WHAT CAN I DO?
WELL, ODIN...I HAVE A BIG FAVOR TO ASK...

RAGHH!!!
IRON MAN TO AVENGERS HQ, THOR IS COMPROMISED! I NEED IMMEDIATE EVAC OR-- OR BACKUP OR... SOMETHING!!!
HELLO? HEY!!! IS ANYONE--?
STOP!
PUNCHING!
FWAP
KRAK
HULK!!!
AGH!!!

COME ON!!! CAN ANYONE HEAR--
ANTHONY STARK...
WE CAN HEAR YOU.
BOOOM
H...RIGHT... HE TALKING BIRDS.
NOW VERYTHING MAKES--
VWAAAMM
--SENSE-- WHOAAA, HEY!!!
SMASH

HAGH! WHERE...? OKAY...
LITTLE WARNING NEXT TIME WOULD BE GREAT!
MY APOLOGIES. I THOUGHT THAT HUGINN AND MUNINN WERE QUITE CLEAR.
WAIT, SIF, THAT WAS YOU? I THOUGHT ONLY--
THOR IS NOT THE ONLY ONE CAPABLE OF SPEAKING THROUGH THE RAVENS. NOW FIND SHELTER.
I AM BRINGING MY KING HOME.
HOLD UP, YOU'RE BRINGING THOR HERE? I DON'T KNOW IF YOU SAW WHAT WAS GOING ON, BUT HE'S NOT QUITE HIMSELF RIGHT NOW.
I SEE EVERYTHING. YES, THOR IS LOST. OUT OF CONTROL.
BUT IF HE MUST BE STOPPED...
...IT WILL BE BY THE SWORD OF ASGARD.

NO...
HOR...
...THOR WILL NOT... FALL--
VWAAAMM
HRRR!!! NO!!!
AGH!!! THIS...THIS IS IMPOSSIBLE!
WHAT'S HAPPENING?!
THE BIFROST... HE'S...
"...HE'S FIGHTING IT!"
LIGHT!!! LIGHT...NO... TAKE...THOR!!!
AGHHH!!!

LEAVE!
THOR!
KRAKKA-DOOOM
ALONE!!

THOR...
...I...I HAVE FAILED YOU...
WAAAA-DOOOM
DOWN!!!

ARE YOU--?
NO...
NO, IT'S NOT POSSIBLE...
HE...
...HE BROKE IT.
THE BIFROST IS NO MORE.

GODS...
HE'S...
...HE'S GONE.
NOT NECESSARILY.
I THINK I CAN STOP HIM.
I JUST NEED--
ABSOLUTELY NOT! I AM NOT AIDING YOU IN YOUR QUEST TO LOSE EVEN MORE OF THAT MIND OF YOURS. WE MUST TRY TO SUBDUE HIM WITH--
YOU DON'T UNDERSTAND. THAT IS NOT THOR.
THIS...THIS NEW THING I HAVE INSIDE OF ME, TITAN... IT POSSESSES PEOPLE. TURNS THEM INTO KILLING MACHINES. HE'S BASICALL A WALKING, TALKING VERSION OF WHAT MADE ME WHAT I AM NOW...
AND IF I TRY TO GO TOE TO TOE WITH THOR OUT THERE...TITAN IS GOING TO COME BACK OUT. AND THEN...THIS ALL ENDS... EVERYTHING.
SO...
...ABOUT THAT FAVOR...

HA! RAINBOW SCARED OF THOR!
RAINBOW RUN AWAY BACK TO--
RMMBBLLL
UGH?
RMMBBBLLL
RMMMMBRRRL
HAMMER! TO--

AGH!!!
KER-SMACK
HAMMER HURT THOR!!!
YOU'D BETTER BE DAMN SURE OF THIS.
WELL...
BOOM
...THERE'S ONLY ONE WAY...
FWAP
...TO FIND OUT!
SMASHA-THOOM

YOU...
...YOU STEAL THOR'S HAMMER!
AYE.

YOU WANT IT BACK?
RAAAGHHHHH!!!
COME AND TAKE IT.
AGHHHHH!!!
RAGHHH!!!

KRAKA-DOOOOOOM

HULK #7 VARIANT BY **LOGAN LUBERA & RACHELLE ROSENBERG**

THOR #26 VARIANT BY **TAURIN CLARKE**

HULK #8 VARIANT BY **TAURIN CLARKE**

HULK #8
BANNER OF WAR PART FIVE
ANDERSON

THE ...ESTION.
THE QUESTION ASKED FOR DECADES PAST AND...SHOULD THE UNIVERSE SURVIVE THIS DAY...
...TO BE DEBATED FOR CENTURIES TO COME.
I...AM UATU. SWORN TO WATCH IN PASSIVE OBSERVATION AS HISTORY'S GREATEST MOMENTS UNRAVEL IN THE FACE OF ETERNITY.
AND HERE, I PRESENT TO YOU...
...THE QUESTION...
...ANSWERED AT LAST...

"WHO...IN A BATTLE TO THE DEATH... WOULD WIN?
"THOR. THE GOD OF THUNDER. THE ALL-FATHER...
"OR HULK? THE STRONGEST ONE THERE IS. THE WORLD BREAKER.
"TODAY, THAT QUESTION WILL BE ANSWERED...
BANNER! GET US TO ASGARD!
YOU KEEP SAYING THAT LIKE I CAN JUST FLY US THERE! HOW CAN I GET THERE IF THOR JUST BROKE YOUR RAINBOW BRIDGE?
BESIDES, NOT SURE IF YOU NOTICED...
"...HOWEVER, AS WITH ALL THINGS...
...I'M A LITTLE OCCUPIED!
YOU DON'T REALLY THINK I'VE GIVEN MJOLNIR TO YOU SO THAT YOU CAN STRUT ABOUT IN ARMOR AND LIGHTNING, DO YOU?
BELIEVE IT OR NOT, BANNER, MY SON OFTEN HOLDS BACK DISPLAYING THE SHEER SCOPE OF MJOLNIR'S POWER.
BUT I. AM NOT SON

"...THE ANSWER WILL COME...
"BEHOLD!!!
"...WITH A PRICE."
"THE BIFROST MAY BE GONE, AYE...
"BUT ASGARD...
"...ASGARD REMAINS."

WAIT, BETA RAY BILL, DO YOU SEE THAT? WHY DOES HULK HAVE--
HOLD!
KRA-KOOOOM
AGH!
STAND, STARK. FOR IT MAY BE YOUR LAST CHANCE TO DO SO.
I DON'T GET IT, SIF. HULK...HE HAS MJOLNIR...
EVEN WITHOUT IT, I MEAN...THOR HAS ON BARELY BEATEN H IN THE PAST. HOW CAN HE--
THAT...
...IS UNTRUE.
THE HULK HAS NEVER FOUGHT THOR.
NO THE R THOR

N THE PAST, WHEN
EY HAVE FOUGHT...
"...HULK FACED THE AVENGER. THE HUMBLE AND NOBLE THOR."
BUT DO NOT FORGET...
...THERE WAS A REASON THOR WAS CAST DOWN TO MIDGARD.
TO LEARN HUMILITY. TO LEARN HONOR.
TO LEARN TO WIELD HIS POWER...WITH MERCY.
T NOW...HULK FACES NOT JUST
MIRROR OF HIS OWN RAGE...
"...BUT A RAGE THAT HAS BEEN HELD BACK FOR HUNDREDS OF YEARS.
"A POWER... THIS WORLD HAS NEVER SEEN.
"IN THE PAST, WHEN THEY HAVE CLASHED... THOR BELIEVED, TRULY IN HIS HEART, THAT SOMEWHERE INSIDE OF THE HULK..."
...THERE WAS A MAN. AN ALLY. A WARRIOR WORTHY OF FORGIVENESS.
"OF MERCY.
"BUT NOW...IF THOR IS TRULY UNLEASHED... IF HE SEES NO MAN INSIDE OF THAT BEAST...

"...HULK WILL FINALLY LEARN...
"...WHAT IT IS TO FIGHT A GOD."
AGHH!!!
DAMMIT, BOY...

RAGHHHH!!!
"THERE! NOW'S OUR CHANCE!"
PUSH HIM INTO YGGDRASIL.
THE WORLD TREE WILL BURN THIS MADNESS OUT OF HIM.
RAAAAGHHH!!!
THOR SM--
KROOM

DOOOOOM
OKAY...I, UH...I PUSHED HIM INTO THE TREE.
IS THAT... IT? IS IT OVER? OR--?
YOU...YOUR MONSTER. IT IS FUELED BY RAGE. YOU SAID IT YOURSELF.
AND YET HERE YOU ARE--IN CONTROL OF THAT MADNESS. YOU HAVE LEARNED TO CAGE IT. TO LET IT FUEL YOU INSTEAD OF CONTROL YOU...
FOR NOW. YES. BUT YOU DIDN'T ANSWER MY--
YOUR BATTLE MAY BE OVER...
"...BUT FOR THOR...RIGHT NOW WE ARE USING THE UNITED POWER OF EVERY REALM IN THE KNOWN AND UNKNOWN UNIVERSE TO CAGE HIS MADNESS...
"ALL OF THE VOICES OF THE ELDERS WHISPERING TO HIM, GUIDING HIM BACK TO THE GOD THAT HE IS...
"ALL OF THE MAGICS AND ENCHANTMENTS KNOWN TO THE RUNES AND FATES TO LEECH THIS FURY FROM HIS SOUL...
"ALL OF THIS...
...AND I...
...I DO THINK ENOUG

AGHHH!!!
HRAAHHH!!!
SNAP
SNAP
RRRRR...
GODS NO...
THOR, PLEASE...
RAAAGHHH!!!

GREAT HEL...
IF HE DOESN'T STOP... WE'RE TALKING THE END OF REALITY. WE'VE GOT TO CALM HIM DOWN.
WHAT COULD WE POSSIBLY DO TO END THIS... MADNESS?
IT MIGHT BE TIME FOR LESS FORCE...
"...AND MORE WORDS."
GRAHHHHGGGG!
VWAVWAVWA
my son!
IT IS I...
...YOU FATHER

IT IS ODIN.
GRUH?
I...I AM SORRY, MY SON. [N]OT ONLY FOR YOUR [MA]NY TROUBLES...BUT [F]OR WHAT I HAVE DONE AS WELL.
I KNOW I HAVE NOT ALWAYS BEEN KIND TO YOU. I HAVE MADE MANY MISTAKES.
TOO MANY.
BUT THROUGH IT ALL, DESPITE MY FAILURES, DESPITE OUR DIFFERENCES...I MUST REMIND YOU...
...I STILL LOVE YOU, SON.
HRAH!
IF YOU WOULD, MY BOY... ALLOW ME TO DO WHAT ALL FATHERS ARE CALLED ON TO DO FOR THEIR SONS:
HELP THEM WITH THEIR BURDENS.

AND RELIEVE THEM OF THEIR WOES.

UNH!
"THAT BLAST, IT KNOCKED ME RIGHT OUT. WHAT HAPPENED IN THERE, THOR? WHERE IS HULK?"
"FRIEND STARK, THE MAGIC WITHIN MJOLNIR WAS ABLE TO REMOVE MY GAMMA AND RESTORE THE WORLD TREE.
"BUT THE RESULTING EXPLOSION OF ENERGY WAS TOO MUCH FOR ALL BUT A GOD TO WITHSTAND..."

"SO THAT MEANS--"
"YES.
"BRUCE BANNER...
"...THE HULK...

"...IS DEAD."
"I CAN'T BELIEVE IT..."

...I CAN'T BELIEVE HE'S GONE.
I THINK IN SOME WAY, BANNER LET HIMSELF BE DESTROYED. HE WANTED TO BE...
...FREE.
AND I WANT TO BE HOME.
AAAA

CRACK
AND SO YOU SHALL BE, MY FRIEND.
SAFE TRAVELS, TONY.
AH!
SO? WHERE IS HE?
FAR FROM HERE. WHERE HE IS GOING, EVEN I CANNOT SEE.
THOR. SHOULD YOU REALLY HAVE LET HIM GO?
BANNER IS NOT TO BLAME FOR WHAT HAPPENED IN EL PASO. BUT HE KNOWS THE WORLD WOULD FOREVER DOUBT HIS INNOCENCE...
I HAVE LIVED BEHIND BANNER'S EYES, SIF. I HAVE FELT HIS RAGE AND HIS PAIN.

"I SHARE IN THOSE THINGS MORE THAN I WISH.
"SO I MUST RESPECT HIS WILL. AND MAYBE SOMEDAY...HE SHALL FIND HEALING AS WELL. HE DESERVES IT.
"WE ALL DO."
THE END...?

CONNECTING VARIANTS BY **GEOFF SHAW & FEDERICO BLEE**

THOR #25 VARIANT BY
J. SCOTT CAMPBELL & SABINE RICH

THOR #25 RETRO VARIANT BY
J. SCOTT CAMPBELL & SABINE RICH

HULK #7 VARIANT BY

HULK #7 RETRO VARIANT BY

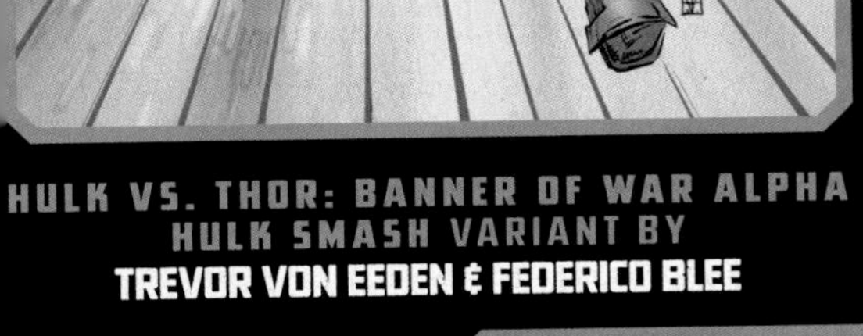

HULK VS. THOR: BANNER OF WAR ALPHA
HULK SMASH VARIANT BY
TREVOR VON EEDEN & FEDERICO BLEE

HULK VS. THOR: BA
MJOLNIR CRA
TREVOR VON EE

HULK #7 SKRULL VARIANT BY **JUNGGEUN YOON**

THOR #26 PRIDE VARIANT BY **BETSY COLA**

HULK #8 HELLFIRE GALA VARIANT BY **RUSSELL DAUTERMAN & MATT WILSON**

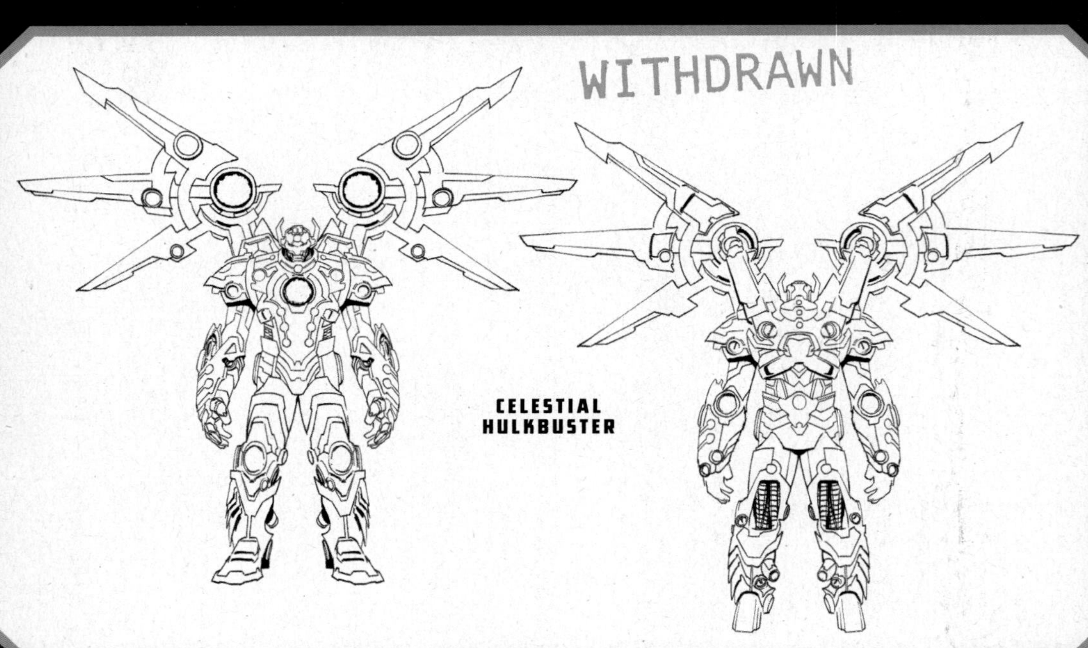

CHARACTER DESIGNS BY MARTIN COCCOLO